NEWSMAKERS

KETANJI BROWN JACKSON
SUPREME COURT JUSTICE

BY AMY C. REA

Core Library
An Imprint of Abdo Publishing
abdobooks.com

Cover image: Ketanji Brown Jackson smiles as she is sworn in for her confirmation hearings as a nominee to the US Supreme Court.

abdobooks.com

Published by Abdo Publishing, a division of ABDO, PO Box 398166, Minneapolis, Minnesota 55439. Copyright © 2023 by Abdo Consulting Group, Inc. International copyrights reserved in all countries. No part of this book may be reproduced in any form without written permission from the publisher. Core Library™ is a trademark and logo of Abdo Publishing.

Printed in the United States of America, North Mankato, Minnesota.
052022
092022

THIS BOOK CONTAINS RECYCLED MATERIALS

Cover Photo: Kevin Lamarque/Getty Images News/Getty Images
Interior Photos: Nathan Posner/Anadolu Agency/Getty Images, 4–5; Al Drago/Bloomberg/Getty Images, 7, 43; Kent Nishimura/Los Angeles Times/Getty Images, 10–11, 18–19; Roman Babakin/Shutterstock Images, 13; J. Scott Applewhite/AP Photo/Bloomberg/Getty Images, 14, 45; Mike Flippo/Shutterstock Images, 20; Robert S. Oakes/Library of Congress, 23; Susan Walsh/AP Images, 26–27; Red Line Editorial, 29; Samuel Corum/Getty Images News/Getty Images, 32–33; Drew Angerer/Getty Images News/Getty Images, 35; Tom Williams/CQ-Roll Call Inc/Getty Images, 36; Justin Sullivan/Getty Images News/Getty Images, 38 (Jackson); Rob Crandall/Shutterstock Images, 38 (Breyer); Saul Loeb/AFP/Getty Images, 38 (Sotomayor); Erin Schaff/Getty Images News/Getty Images, 38 (Kagan), 38 (Barrett); Mehdi Kasumov/Shutterstock Images, 41

Editor: Angela Lim
Series Designer: Katharine Hale

Library of Congress Control Number: 2022936011

Publisher's Cataloging-in-Publication Data

Names: Rea, Amy C., author.
Title: Ketanji Brown Jackson: supreme court justice / by Amy C. Rea
Other Title: supreme court justice
Description: Minneapolis, Minnesota: Abdo Publishing, 2023 | Series: Newsmakers | Includes online resources and index.
Identifiers: ISBN 9781532199172 (lib. bdg.) | ISBN 9781098273187 (ebook)
Subjects: LCSH: Jackson, Ketanji Brown, 1970---Juvenile literature. | Women judges--United States--Biography--Juvenile literature. | Supreme Court justices--Biography--Juvenile literature. | UnitedStates.--Supreme Court--Officials and employees--Biography--Juvenile literature.
Classification: DDC 347.73--dc23

CONTENTS

CHAPTER ONE
A Lawyer from the Start 4

CHAPTER TWO
Early Life and Education 10

CHAPTER THREE
A Lawyer and a Public Defender ...18

CHAPTER FOUR
Judge Jackson 26

CHAPTER FIVE
The Supreme Court 32

Important Dates......................42

Stop and Think......................44

Glossary 46

Online Resources 47

Learn More 47

Index 48

About the Author 48

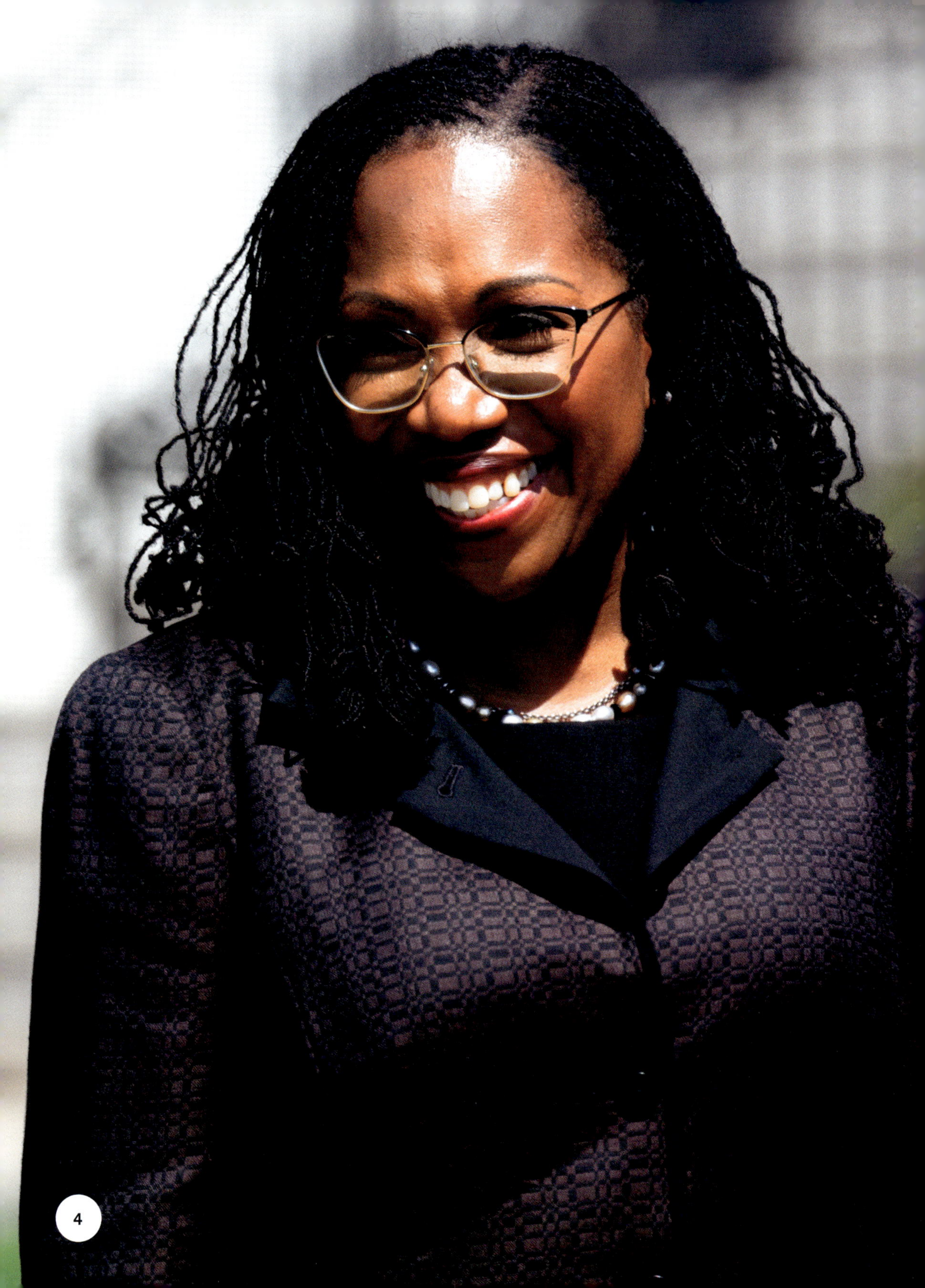

CHAPTER ONE

A LAWYER FROM THE START

It was April 7, 2022. Ketanji Brown Jackson was at the White House in Washington, DC. It was one of the most important days in Jackson's life. She watched a TV along with President Joe Biden and several news reporters.

Biden had nominated Jackson for the Supreme Court on February 25, 2022. Jackson needed to go through multiple steps before becoming a Supreme Court justice. She went through several days of interviews

Ketanji Brown Jackson smiled as she celebrated her confirmation to the Supreme Court.

WHY A DIVERSE SUPREME COURT IS IMPORTANT

The United States has a diverse population. Having a Supreme Court that reflects the population is important. A diverse court includes justices of different backgrounds. Their experiences may influence how they interpret the US Constitution. The justices may have different insights about the cases before them. They may rule differently from one another based on their backgrounds. A diverse court also increases trust. People are more likely to trust the courts when they feel represented and understood.

with senators. Now the Senate was voting to confirm her nomination. She would soon learn if her lifelong dream of being on the Supreme Court would come true.

Jackson needed a majority of the senators to vote for her. The US Senate has 100 members. She would be confirmed as a justice if she received 51 votes. As the senators voted, the TV showed the number of yes and no votes. The vote was close. But it was expected to pass. Enough senators had publicly said they would vote for her.

Ketanji Brown Jackson delivered a speech on April 8, 2022, after being confirmed to the US Supreme Court.

After about an hour of voting, it was official. The fifty-first vote had been counted in Jackson's favor. Jackson would be sworn in as the next US Supreme Court justice. Biden hugged Jackson in congratulations. Becoming a Supreme Court justice is a high honor. But Jackson's confirmation was an important milestone for other reasons. She would be the first Black woman to sit on the Supreme Court.

The next day, there was a celebration on the South Lawn at the White House. Jackson gave a speech. She thanked her parents and her daughters. She talked about the historic moment. She was proud to be the first Black female justice in the court's 232-year history.

Jackson had dedicated her life to public service because of her love for the United States.

THE HIGHEST COURT IN THE LAND

Being a Supreme Court justice is a lifetime appointment. This means justices can remain on the Supreme Court for the rest of their lives once they have been appointed. Some justices retire. Justice Stephen Breyer announced his retirement in January 2022. Other justices work until the end of their lives. Justice Ruth Bader Ginsburg served on the Supreme Court from 1993 until her death in 2020.

Jackson became the third Black person to serve on the Supreme Court. Thurgood Marshall was the first Black person to serve. He was on the Supreme Court from 1967 until he retired in 1991. Clarence Thomas replaced him. He was the second Black man to serve. Thomas was still on the Supreme Court in 2022.

The Supreme Court reviews the decisions of lower courts. It is the highest court in the land. Only the

Supreme Court can overturn a previous Supreme Court ruling. A Supreme Court justice uses the US Constitution to make rulings. Justices may view the Constitution differently. Some take an originalist approach. They focus on the text of the Constitution. They try to rule as the authors of the Constitution would. Others believe the Constitution is a living document. They take present-day factors into account. The president considers these approaches when making a Supreme Court nomination.

> **SUPREME COURT STATISTICS**
>
> Jackson became the 116th Supreme Court justice in US history. She was only the sixth female justice in US history. There had been four white women and one Hispanic woman on the Supreme Court. Of the remaining justices, all but two were white men. As of 2022, Jackson was the second-youngest person appointed to the Supreme Court. She was 51 years old when she was confirmed.

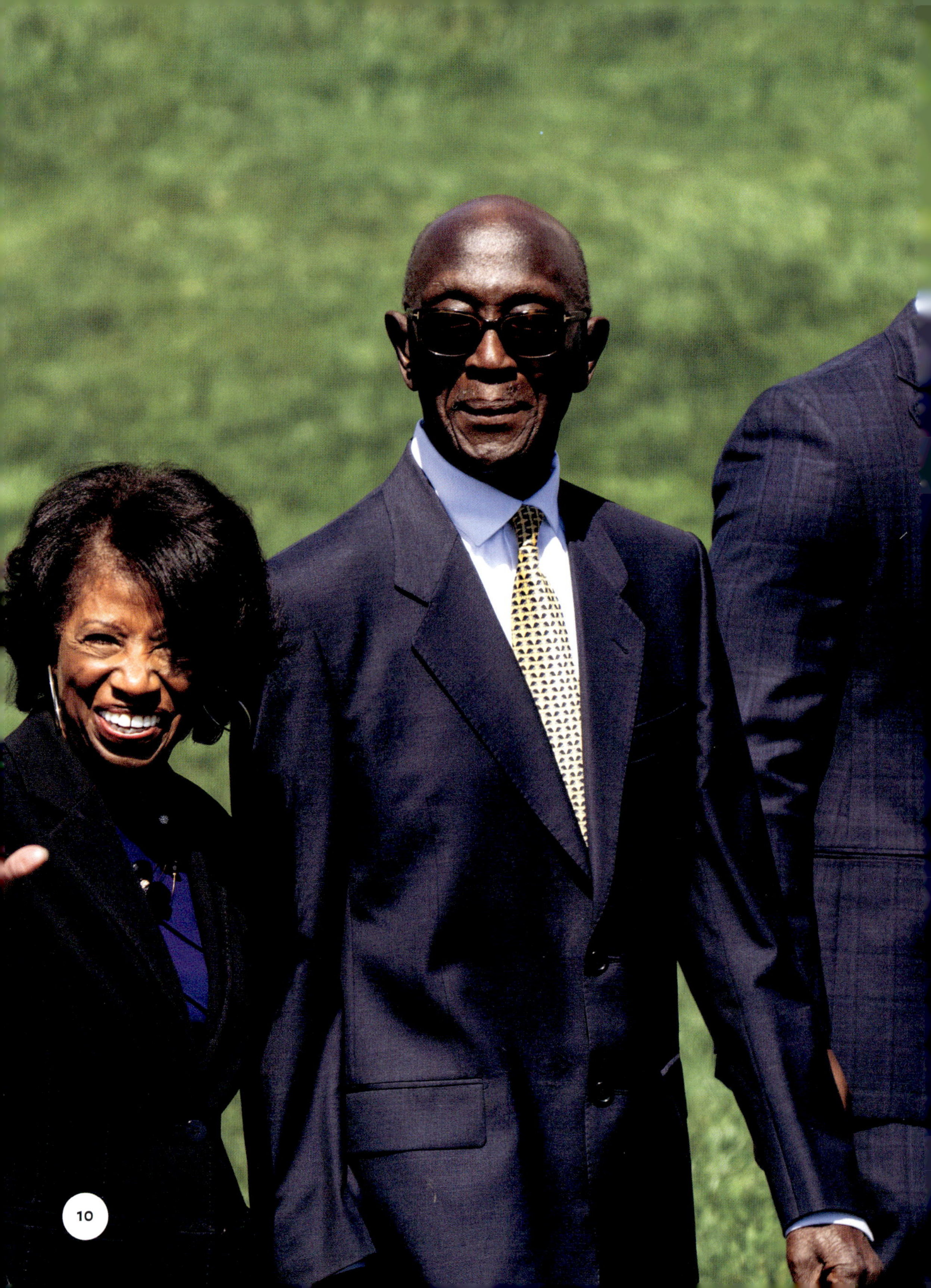

CHAPTER
TWO

EARLY LIFE AND EDUCATION

Ketanji Brown was born on September 14, 1970, in Washington, DC, to Johnny and Ellery Brown. The Browns wanted to honor their African ancestry. They asked a friend who was serving in the Peace Corps in West Africa for a list of African names. They chose Ketanji Onyika.

Both of Ketanji's parents were teachers. They attended segregated schools when they were young. The Browns moved to Miami after

Jackson's parents, Ellery and Johnny, and brother Ketajh, *left to right*, celebrated Jackson's confirmation on the White House lawn.

11

Ketanji's birth. Ketanji's father studied at the University of Miami Law School. Ketanji would sit at the kitchen table with her coloring books while her father studied his law books. Later, Jackson said these moments marked her first interest in the law. Ketanji's younger brother, Ketajh, also followed in their father's footsteps. Ketajh grew up to be a lawyer.

Ketanji was raised in Miami. While attending Miami Palmetto Senior High School, Ketanji was elected student body president. She was involved in speech and debate. This experience gave her self-confidence. It also taught her how to persevere despite obstacles. Her high school education prepared her with reasoning and writing skills. These skills proved to be valuable in her future career as a lawyer and judge.

EARLY DETERMINATION

Ketanji showed an interest in law while she was still in high school. She is quoted in her senior-year yearbook. She said she wanted to become a judge.

Jackson attended Harvard University in Cambridge, Massachusetts.

Ketanji believed that attending Harvard University would help her achieve her career goals. But her guidance counselor suggested that Jackson should not set her sights so high. Ketanji did not take that advice. She applied to Harvard and was accepted. She began her college career in 1988.

Jackson sits with her husband Patrick, *left*, and her two daughters during her confirmation hearing.

Ketanji demonstrated her leadership at Harvard. Some students hung a Confederate flag from a dorm window. The flag represented the South during the American Civil War (1861–1865). Southern states fought to keep slavery legal. Black students felt the flag meant that they were not welcome at Harvard. But the university decided it did not have the power to tell students to take down the flag.

Black students protested the decision. Some skipped classes to protest. Ketanji joined the protests. But she said that protesting and education were both important. They could fail courses if they skipped classes. If they failed, others could say the failures proved Black students did not belong at Harvard. She saw both the need to protest and to protect their futures.

Ketanji earned a bachelor's degree in government from Harvard in 1992. She graduated *magna cum laude*, Latin for "with

DR. PATRICK JACKSON

Ketanji was in her family's second generation of college graduates. Her husband, Patrick Jackson, was a sixth-generation Harvard graduate. He has a twin brother who also graduated from Harvard. Patrick attended medical school at Columbia University in New York City. When Ketanji was confirmed to the Supreme Court, Patrick was a surgeon at MedStar Georgetown University Hospital.

> **THE BAR EXAM**
>
> Earning a law degree is a big step toward becoming a lawyer. Lawyers must also pass the bar exam before practicing law. This exam tests the person's knowledge of the law. It can take two days to complete. Each US state offers a different bar exam.
>
> Bar associations also prepare evaluations of Supreme Court justice nominees. They issue opinions as to whether the person is qualified. The New York Bar Association found Jackson to be highly qualified for the position.

great distinction." While at Harvard, she met Patrick Jackson. They started dating and later married in 1996. Ketanji changed her name to Ketanji Brown Jackson.

In 1993, she returned to Harvard to attend law school. While in law school, Jackson became an editor for the *Harvard Law Review*. In 1996, she graduated *cum laude*, meaning "with distinction." It was time for Jackson's legal career to begin.

STRAIGHT TO THE
SOURCE

Jackson talked about her parents during her Supreme Court confirmation hearings. She spoke about how she was raised to believe that she could do anything. In her statement to Congress, she said:

> My parents taught me that, unlike the many barriers that they had had to face growing up, my path was clearer, such that if I worked hard and believed in myself, in America I could do anything or be anything I wanted to be. Like so many families in this country, they worked long hours and sacrificed to provide their children every opportunity to reach their God-given potential.
>
> Source: "READ: Ketanji Brown Jackson's Opening Statement at Her Supreme Court Confirmation Hearing." *CNN*, 21 Mar. 2022, cnn.com. Accessed 4 Apr. 2022.

WHAT'S THE BIG IDEA?

Take a close look at this passage. What is the main connection being made between Jackson's childhood and where she is today? How have Jackson's parents influenced her career? What can you tell about the values her parents instilled in her during her childhood?

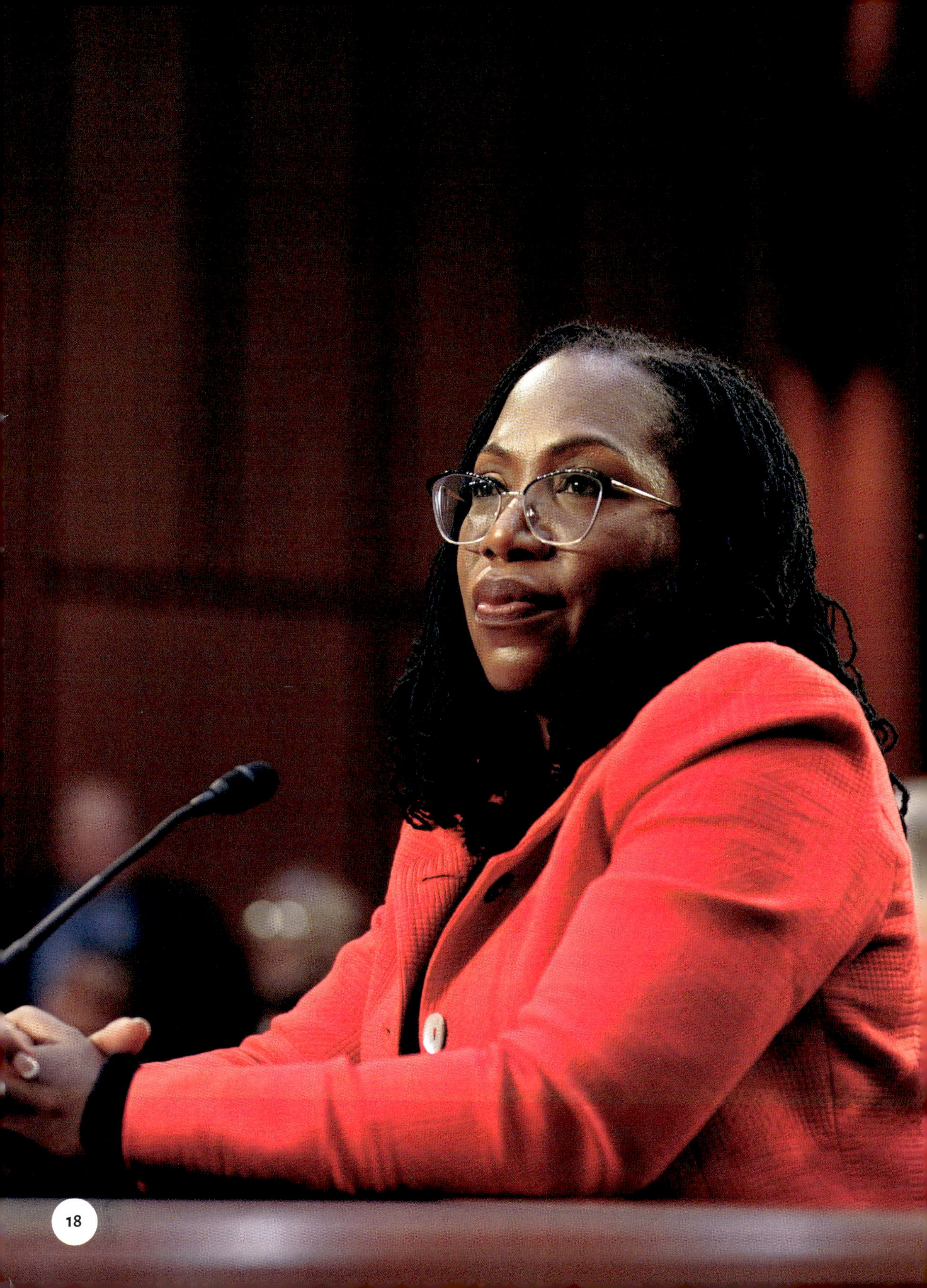

CHAPTER
THREE

A LAWYER AND A PUBLIC DEFENDER

From 1996 to 2003, Jackson worked as a law clerk and an associate in private law practices. She alternated between these positions about every two years during this period. A law clerk is someone who assists a judge in their work. This can involve doing research and checking facts for cases. A law clerk may also communicate with lawyers about cases or help the judge in the courtroom. In 2000, Jackson's first daughter, Talia, was born. Jackson also began clerking for

Jackson listens to questions from senators during her confirmation hearing.

Jackson's early experiences in law helped her better understand the importance of the Constitution.

Justice Stephen Breyer that year. He was the justice that Jackson was later nominated to replace. She left that position in the same year to work as an associate in a private law firm, Goodwin Procter LLP.

Associates are lawyers who work for another lawyer or law firm. Jackson gained experience as an associate. She worked in criminal and civil cases. Criminal cases involve people who have broken the law. Civil cases include money and property disagreements. During part of her career as an associate, Jackson worked with the law firm Morrison & Foerster on Supreme Court cases.

Working for lawyers and judges provided Jackson with experience on both sides of the courtroom. It helped her refine the research, writing, and critical thinking skills she had developed in high school and college. While serving as a law clerk for Breyer, she discovered how important it was for judges to understand the Constitution. Supreme Court justices need to rule fairly. They must be consistent with how they view the Constitution. Jackson also learned how to speak about the Constitution clearly and concisely.

In 2003, Jackson took a detour from clerking and working in private law. That year she joined the US Sentencing Commission as assistant counsel. This commission studies the sentences that are handed out in federal courts. It also develops policies for sentencing. In a courtroom, judges give out a sentence to someone who has been found guilty of a crime. Sentences can include fines, jail time, probation, or community service. Congress created the commission in 1984 to examine sentences. It wanted to make sure similar crimes receive similar punishments. The commission also issues sentencing guidelines to judges. While working for the US Sentencing Commission in 2004, Jackson gave birth to her second daughter, Leila.

Jackson left the commission in 2005. She started a job as an assistant federal public defender. She worked in this position until 2007. A public defender is a lawyer who assists criminal defendants who cannot afford a lawyer. Public defenders do not get to choose who they defend. The court assigns them to defendants. The government pays them.

Public defense was an unusual path

BALANCING WORK AND FAMILY

Jackson and her husband needed to balance demanding careers with the needs of their two children. Jackson talked about this challenge in her opening statement to the Senate. She mentioned her daughters. She knew it was not easy for them as she pursued her career. Jackson said she hoped they had learned what could be accomplished with hard work and love.

Thurgood Marshall served on the Supreme Court for 24 years.

for Jackson. She wanted to become a judge. But very few public defenders go on to become judges. Thurgood Marshall was the only Supreme Court justice to have experience working with criminal defendants. Jackson would later become the first public defender on the Supreme Court. One reason for this is because people can have negative opinions about public defenders. They may believe public defenders are soft on crime. Rulings against defendants may be unfair or harsh. Public defenders help reduce sentences for their defendants. Others may believe that the world is less safe when defendants get lighter sentences.

A JOB AND RIGHT PROTECTED BY THE CONSTITUTION

The US Constitution creates the job of public defender. The Sixth Amendment describes the position. It says that an accused person has the right to legal counsel, even if he or she cannot afford a lawyer. It also says that an accused person has the right to a speedy and public trial with a jury.

Jackson worked on appeals cases as a public defender. These cases involve people who have been convicted of a crime. They appeal to try to get a reduced sentence. Jackson learned that many people did not understand the legal process. She realized it was important to educate her clients. This would help them learn why their actions were wrong. Jackson felt her clients were more likely to continue criminal behavior without education. Her time as a public defender gave her a new perspective on the legal process. She was more empathetic toward people being tried in the justice system.

Having a public defender on the Supreme Court can bring a new perspective to the court. It can give insight into what people in the criminal justice system go through. This can inform decisions made by other justices and allow them to see more sides of trials and legal matters.

EXPLORE ONLINE

Chapter Three discusses Jackson's role as a public defender. The website below goes into more detail about what it means to have a former public defender on the Supreme Court. Why is the perspective of a public defender important? How are public defenders viewed in comparison with other types of lawyers? Why do you think they are viewed in this way?

A PUBLIC DEFENDER ON THE HIGH COURT

abdocorelibrary.com/ketanji-brown-jackson

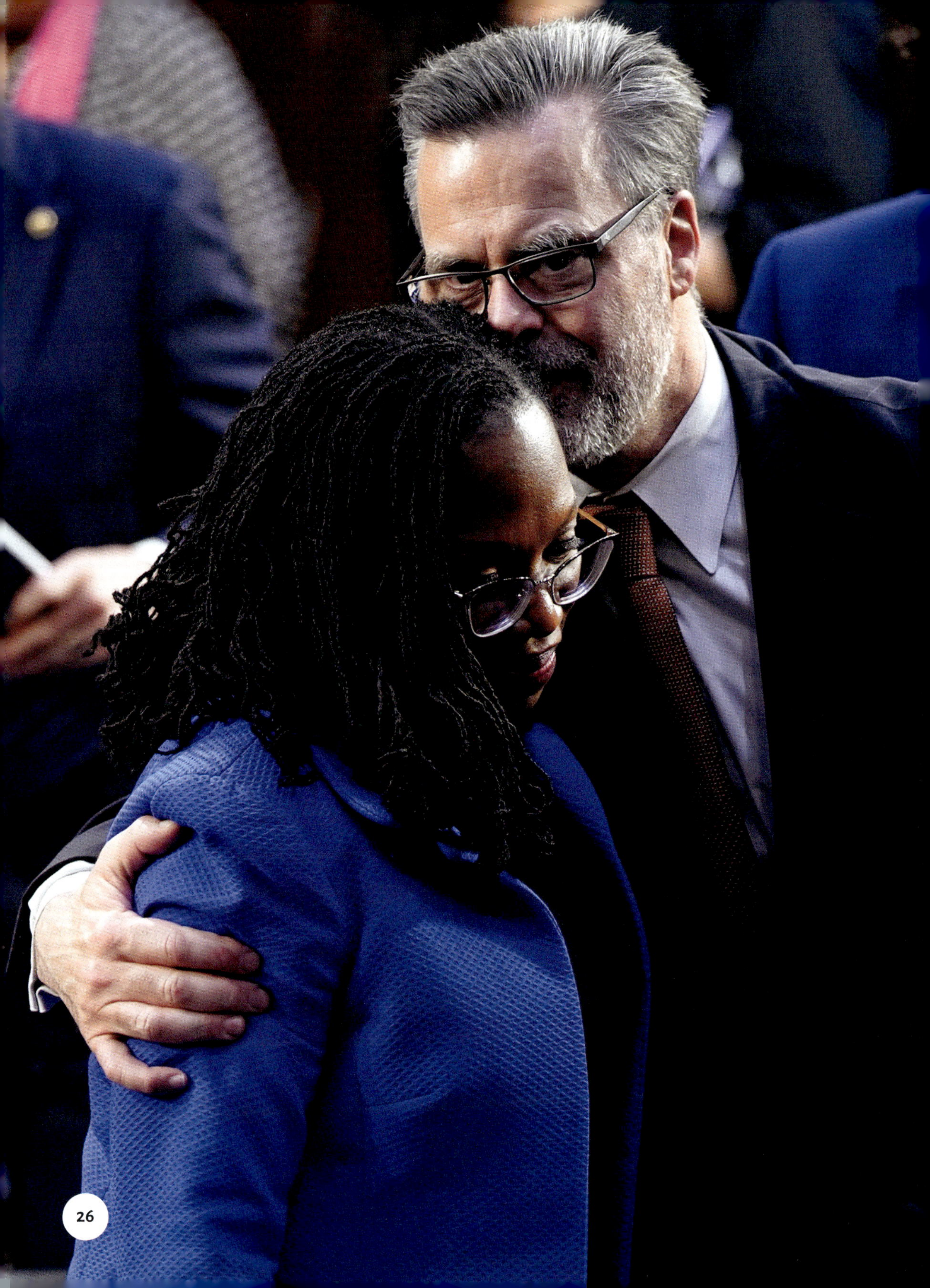

CHAPTER FOUR

JUDGE JACKSON

Jackson was working for the US Sentencing Commission on September 20, 2012. That day, President Barack Obama nominated her to the US District Court for Washington, DC. However, Congress adjourned before voting on her nomination. Obama nominated her again when Congress was back in session in 2013. On March 23, 2013, the Senate voted to confirm her appointment. Jackson had reached her goal of becoming a judge.

Jackson's husband showed continued support of her judicial pursuits.

27

BECOMING A JUDGE

Most states require judges to have a law degree. Experience in a courtroom can also help someone be appointed as a judge. Judges need many skills to be successful. They should be good at communication. They should be able to listen to both sides of an argument without bias. They should be able to stay calm under pressure.

In her eight years on the district court, Jackson gave rulings on several important cases. One case in 2013 involved a young man who had committed a felony. Federal guidelines called for up to ten years in prison. The prosecutor asked for two years. The defense attorney asked for one day in jail and five years of supervised release. The defendant was young and had no prior offenses. Jackson ruled that the defendant would spend three months in prison. Then he would spend three months in home detention and six years in supervised release.

One of Jackson's most famous cases on the district court was in 2019. Don McGahn, a former attorney

HIGHER COURT RULINGS ON APPEALED CASES JUDGED BY JACKSON

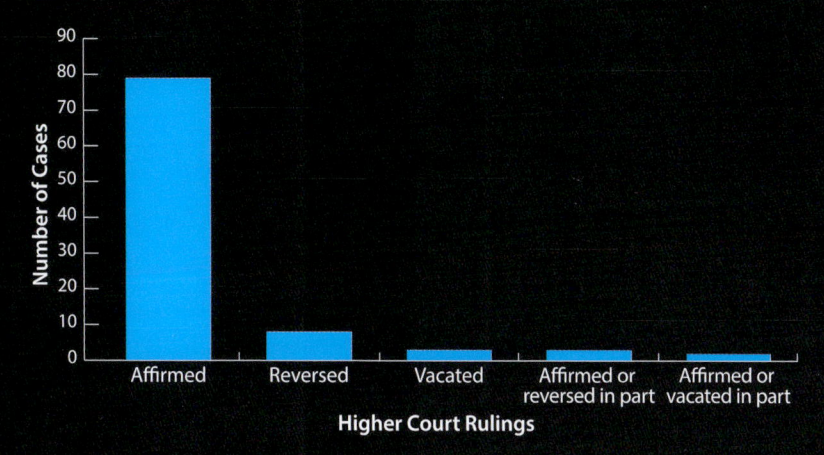

Judges on higher courts may agree with, or affirm, the ruling from a district court. If the higher court strongly disagrees with a ruling, it reverses the decision. It can also choose to vacate the ruling. This is done when the higher court believes the ruling was only somewhat incorrect.

for President Donald Trump, was required to testify before a congressional committee. He was to speak about Russia's interference in the 2016 presidential election and Trump's possible obstruction of justice in that matter. Trump told McGahn not to appear before Congress. So McGahn refused to testify. He stated that only the president should decide who should testify. Jackson ruled against him. She said Congress and the courts had the right to order him to testify.

MAKE MY MOM A JUDGE

When Jackson's daughter Leila was 11 years old, she wrote a letter to Obama. She asked him to nominate her mother for the Supreme Court. Obama chose Merrick Garland instead. Garland was a judge on the US Court of Appeals at the time. But the Senate did not confirm Garland. Biden became president in 2021. He selected Garland to be the US attorney general. This created an opening in the Court of Appeals. Biden nominated Jackson to fill the position.

In 2021, Jackson was promoted to the US Court of Appeals, which reviews rulings that are made in lower courts. It is often referred to as the second-highest court in the land. In her years as a judge, Jackson worked on many cases involving congressional investigations, labor rights, immigration issues, and more. These cases provided her with experience on many legal topics and would help her in her next big chapter.

STRAIGHT TO THE SOURCE

Jackson ruled on the 2019 McGahn case while serving on the district court. She ruled that McGahn was required to testify before Congress. In her ruling, she said:

> *The primary takeaway from the past 250 years of recorded American history is that presidents are not kings. . . . This means that they do not have subjects, bound by loyalty or blood, whose destiny they are entitled to control. Rather, in this land of liberty . . . [White House employees] work for the People of the United States [and] take an oath to protect and defend the Constitution of the United States.*
>
> Source: "Don McGahn Ruling." *Associated Press*, 25 Nov. 2019, documentcloud.org. Accessed 11 Apr. 2022.

CONSIDER YOUR AUDIENCE

Review this passage closely. Consider how you would adapt it for a different audience, such as your parents, your principal, or younger friends. Write a blog post conveying this same information for the new audience. How does your new approach differ from the original text and why?

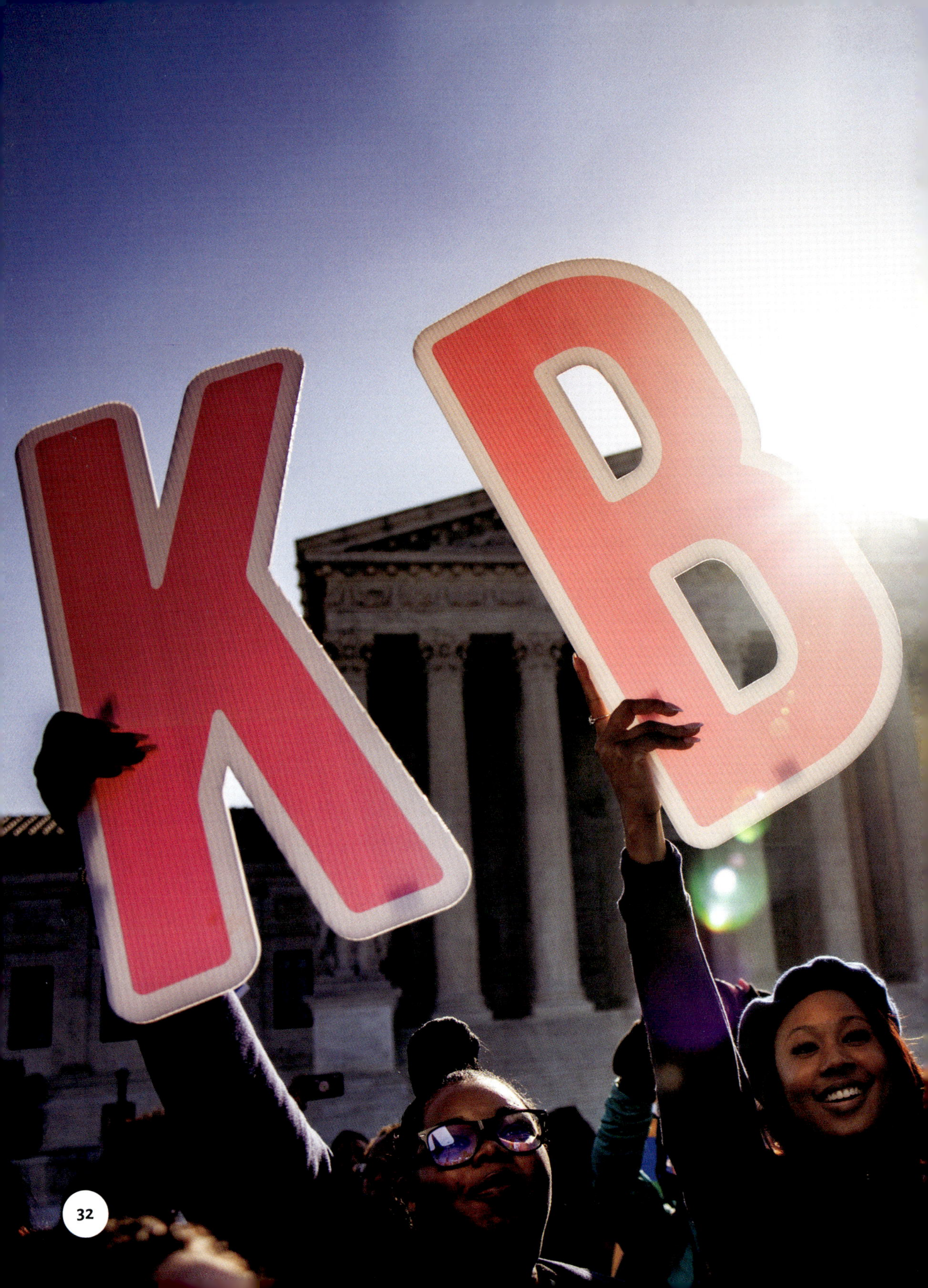
K
B

CHAPTER FIVE

THE SUPREME COURT

Stephen Breyer announced his retirement from the Supreme Court in January 2022. On February 25, President Joe Biden nominated Jackson to fill Breyer's position. Her nomination had to be confirmed by the Senate. The first step was confirmation hearings. Senators would question Jackson. They would make sure Jackson was qualified and would rule fairly. The next step was Senate Judiciary Committee hearings. The committee was made up of

Jackson's supporters stand outside of the Supreme Court to celebrate her nomination.

22 senators. They decide whether the vote should continue to the full Senate. Finally all 100 senators would vote on whether to approve the nomination.

Confirmation hearings can be stressful. The hearings took place over four days, beginning on March 21. Jackson was present and questioned for the first three days. The process began with Jackson giving an opening statement. Then the floor was open for senators to ask her questions. The second and third days of the hearings each lasted for more than ten hours. Dozens of cameras pointed at Jackson throughout the process. The hearings were broadcast on live television and the internet.

Senators asked Jackson about her approach as a judge. They wanted to know how she interpreted the Constitution. Many justices do not define their methods during their confirmation hearings. Likewise Jackson did not give specifics about her approach.

Some senators worried about Jackson's approach as a judge. They were worried she would be soft

Stephen Breyer, whom Jackson clerked for, announced his retirement from the Supreme Court on January 27, 2022.

on criminals. They talked about the 2013 felony case she ruled on while on the district court. Jackson had given a shorter sentence than what the prosecutor had asked for. The defendant appeared in her courtroom again in 2019. Some senators wondered if the man had committed a similar crime. They asked if Jackson

Jackson meets with Republican senator John Kennedy, *center*, and Owen Stokes, *left*, the son of Kennedy's chief of staff.

regretted shortening the prison term. Jackson defended her decision. She talked about her role as a judge. She said the sentence was consistent with the law and federal requirements.

Some senators questioned Jackson about race relations. Senator Ted Cruz asked questions about Jackson's views on critical race theory. Critical race theory explains how racism has shaped society and legal systems. Cruz asked whether Jackson believes that every conflict is a result of racism. She answered that she has never studied critical race theory. She said that it does not come up in her work as a judge.

NUMBER OF JUSTICES

As of 2022, the Supreme Court includes nine justices. It has been that way since 1869. But the number has changed throughout US history. The Supreme Court was first established in 1789. It had six justices. Between 1789 and 1869, the number of active justices changed six times. It has ranged from five to ten justices.

Senator Dick Durbin raised a question about the size of the Supreme Court. At the time of Jackson's nomination, the court had nine members. President Biden had put together a commission to study the possibility of increasing the number to 13. Former Supreme Court Justice Ruth Bader Ginsburg disagreed with this idea. Some senators also did not approve.

A HIGHLY QUALIFIED NOMINEE

Jackson replaced Breyer on the Supreme Court. She joined three other female justices. Jackson shares experiences with these justices. But she also brings unique qualifications to the position.

Supreme Court Justices

Credentials	Ketanji Brown Jackson	Stephen Breyer	Sonia Sotomayor	Elena Kagan	Amy Coney Barrett
Public high school	✓	✓		✓	
Ivy League law school	✓	✓	✓	✓	
Supreme Court clerking	✓			✓	✓
Public defender	✓				
Sentencing commission	✓	✓			
District judge	✓		✓		
Court of Appeals judge	✓	✓	✓		✓

Biden could nominate liberal judges to the new positions if the court were expanded. This would change the way the Supreme Court rules for many years. Durbin asked Jackson what her opinion was on the matter. Jackson declined to answer. She said it was not appropriate for a judge to comment on political matters.

Members of the American Bar Association (ABA) were present for the hearing. The ABA is an organization for lawyers. On the last day of the hearings, three ABA members talked about Jackson's qualifications. They confirmed that she was qualified to be a Supreme Court justice. Then Democrats and Republicans called on several witnesses. They gave their final thoughts about Jackson as a potential Supreme Court justice.

On April 4, 2022, the Senate Judiciary Committee voted on whether Jackson's nomination should continue forward. The committee is bipartisan. The vote was tied, 11 to 11. Democrats called for the full Senate to vote

A PARTISAN ISSUE

Supreme Court nominations are partisan issues. Democrats and Republicans often disagree about who should be nominated to the Supreme Court. They support a justice who they believe represents the ideals of their party. Since Biden is a Democratic president, Republicans did not want to approve Jackson's nomination. Similarly, Democrats worked to block Trump's nominations since he was a Republican.

on whether Jackson's nomination should be moved to the full Senate. The Senate voted for the process to continue. On April 7, the full Senate approved Jackson with a vote of 53 to 47.

Jackson achieved a life goal by being appointed to the Supreme Court. Her education and years as a federal judge would help her as a Supreme Court justice. She would also bring a unique perspective to the court with her experience as a public defender. Jackson's appointment was also a historic moment for the United States. Jackson would be the first Black

The Supreme Court Building is just one of many iconic white marble buildings in Washington, DC.

woman on the Supreme Court. She represented another step toward equality. She inspired many to work hard for their dreams.

FURTHER EVIDENCE

Chapter Five discusses how some senators were concerned about Jackson's views on critical race theory. The website below goes into more detail about what critical race theory is and why some senators worry about it. Does the information on the website support the information in this chapter about critical race theory? Does it provide new evidence?

WHY ARE STATES BANNING CRITICAL RACE THEORY?
abdocorelibrary.com/ketanji-brown-jackson

IMPORTANT DATES

1970
Ketanji Brown is born to Johnny and Ellery Brown in Washington, DC, on September 14. Both of her parents are teachers at this time.

1996
Brown graduates *cum laude* from Harvard Law School. She begins her first legal job as a law clerk. She marries Patrick Jackson and changes her name to Ketanji Brown Jackson.

2000
Jackson starts working for the private law firm Goodwin Procter LLP.

2003
Jackson begins working at the US Sentencing Commission.

2005
Jackson takes a position as a public defender.

2013
Jackson becomes a judge for the US District Court for Washington, DC.

2021
Jackson is promoted as a judge for the US Court of Appeals.

February 25, 2022
President Joe Biden nominates Jackson to become a Supreme Court justice.

March 21–24, 2022
The US Senate holds confirmation hearings and interviews Jackson for the Supreme Court.

April 7, 2022
The US Senate votes 53 to 47 to confirm Jackson's nomination to the Supreme Court. She replaces Justice Stephen Breyer upon his retirement later that year.

STOP AND
THINK

Tell the Tale
Chapter Two talks about protests at Harvard University due to students hanging a Confederate flag from a dorm window. Imagine you were at Harvard when these protests occurred. How would you support Black students? What would you say to the students who wanted to protest?

Take a Stand
One reason that Jackson is a groundbreaker in her Supreme Court appointment is that she is the first justice to have worked as a public defender. Why is that important? Do you think more Supreme Court justices should have experience as public defenders? Why or why not?

Why Do I Care?
Maybe you are not interested in becoming a Supreme Court justice or working in law. But you might have friends and family who are interested. What could you tell them about Jackson's experience? What could they do in their own lives to make the dream a reality?

You Are There

This book discusses Jackson watching the Senate vote to confirm her as a Supreme Court justice. Imagine you are there with her at that historic moment. Write a letter home telling your friends what you saw. What did you notice about Jackson and the feelings in the room? Be sure to add plenty of detail to your notes.

GLOSSARY

adjourn
to stop until a later time

bias
a favoring of a person or point of view over another

bipartisan
relating to the cooperation of two major political parties

convict
to find guilty of a crime in a court of law

defendant
a person accused of a crime

felony
a very serious category of crime

partisan
relating to a strong devotion to a political party, faction, or cause

probation
a period of time when a prisoner is released from prison but is still supervised by an officer

prosecutor
a lawyer who argues for the punishment of the defendant

segregate
to separate based on factors such as race

ONLINE RESOURCES

To learn more about Ketanji Brown Jackson and the Supreme Court, visit our free resource websites below.

Core Library Connection
FREE! COMMON CORE MULTIMEDIA RESOURCES

Visit **abdocorelibrary.com** or scan this QR code for free Common Core resources for teachers and students, including vetted activities, multimedia, and booklinks, for deeper subject comprehension.

Booklinks Nonfiction Network
FREE! ONLINE NONFICTION RESOURCES

Visit **abdobooklinks.com** or scan this QR code for free additional online weblinks for further learning. These links are routinely monitored and updated to provide the most current information available.

LEARN MORE

Abramson, Jill. *What Is the Supreme Court?* Penguin Workshop, 2022.

Kanefield, Teri. *Thurgood Marshall.* Abrams, 2020.

INDEX

bar association, 16, 39
Biden, Joe, 5, 7, 30, 33, 37, 39, 40
Breyer, Stephen, 8, 20–21, 33, 38

Coney Barrett, Amy, 38
confirmation hearings, 17, 33–39
confirmation vote, 6–7, 27, 34, 39–40
Constitution, US, 6, 9, 21, 24, 31, 34
Court of Appeals, US, 30, 38
critical race theory, 36–37, 41

daughters, 7, 19, 22, 30
District Court, US, 27–29, 31, 35, 38

Harvard University, 13–16

Jackson, Patrick, 15, 16, 22

law associates, 19–20
law clerks, 19–21, 38

Marshall, Thurgood, 8, 23
McGahn, Don, 28–29, 31

Obama, Barack, 27, 30

parents, 7, 11–12, 17
public defenders, 22–25, 38, 40

Sentencing Commission, US, 21–22, 27, 38
Supreme Court nomination, 5–6, 9, 16, 20, 33–34, 37–40

Trump, Donald, 29, 40

About the Author

Amy C. Rea grew up in northern Minnesota and now lives in a Minneapolis suburb with her family. She writes frequently about traveling around Minnesota and loves to spend time with her dog.